THE HIDDEN BOX
A Canal Adventure

by Iris Bryce

Best wishes to Sophie,
Iris Bryce
1995

A Belmont Book

"THE HIDDEN BOX" Copyright (1979) Iris Bryce

By the same author:
CANAL BOAT COOKERY 1979
CANALS ARE MY HOME 1979, 1992 (Large print edition 1991)
CANALS ARE MY LIFE 1982 (Large print edition 1993)
CANALS ARE MY WORLD 1986
HIDDEN BOX, THE 1994

Front cover design by Jean Brailsford

All rights reserved. No part of this publication may be reproduced, stored in a retrieval system, or transmitted, in any form or by any means, electronic, mechanical, photocopying, recording or otherwise, without the prior permission in writing of the publishers and the copyright holders.

Printed for and
Published in Great Britain by

THE BELMONT PRESS
29 Tenby Avenue
HARROW HA3 8RU
081-907 4700
FAX 081-907 7354

"THE HIDDEN BOX"   ISBN 0 905366 30 1

I dedicate this story to Erica, Dylan, Lewis, Tanis, Benjamin, Daniel, Paul and Richard — my grandchildren who shared many adventures with me on my narrow boat *Bix*.

CHAPTER ONE

Bev's father swung the blue hold-all up into the rack, his mother made sure for the umpteenth time that he had a clean handkerchief in his pocket, some money for a drink, his comics, and that he knew where the lavatories were on the train.

Bev nodded and smiled back at her, but deep inside he wished so desperately that she would stop fussing — after all he was nine years old, nearly ten, and he was perfectly capable of travelling by himself. He felt a surge of excitement in his stomach at the thought of being in a train for over two hours all by himself. Well, not exactly alone as he now noticed a lady and gentleman who were sitting at the other side of the carriage, but they were both behind newspapers already so he could pretend they were not there quite easily.

His mother however was pleased to see that her son would have travelling companions and she went over to them.

'Excuse me,' she said, 'my son is going to Stoke-on-Trent and I wondered . . . .'

The newspapers were lowered and Bev felt two pairs of eyes turned in his direction. The man rose.

'We're going right through to Manchester and we'll be very pleased to have the young man with us, Mr and Mrs Jackson.' He introduced himself and his wife. Bev's father had now joined them and they all shook hands. Bev wasn't pleased however, but before any more explanations could be given a whistle sounded and there were hugs and kisses and hurried goodbyes from his parents.

'Have a lovely time, be a good boy and give our love to Uncle Peter and Aunt Jean — don't fall in the canal....'

The last remark was said with a laugh as the train slowly pulled out. Bev stood waving goodbye until the dusky gloom of the station gave way to brilliant sunshine. He had forgotten it was still daytime and with surprise he saw the blue sky, the twinkling reflections in hundreds of windows, and people hurrying up and down the streets as the train gathered speed through London.

Factories, warehouses and narrow streets with houses huddled close together flew past the windows for the first few miles and then almost before Bev had settled himself down with his comics he noticed that the houses were spread out more, the roads were wider and he could see grass, trees and fields in between the towns.

Looking through his comics he found that the adventures printed before him became blurred and thoughts of what lay ahead of him eventually took over — he, Bev, was starting out on an adventure! He was going to stay for a whole month with Uncle Peter and Aunt Jean and they lived on a boat! A narrow boat on the canals. Uncle Peter was an artist and he painted pictures which were sold to people who visited the boat — it was in fact a floating art gallery as well as their home. And they travelled constantly up and down the canals and rivers in England.

Bev had never been on a canal boat but his father had shown him some pictures and in every one there had been fields, trees, woods — super places for games and adventures....

'I hope I find someone to play with. I wonder if Aunt Jean knows....'

'Did you speak?'

Bev realised that he had indeed spoken aloud.

'Yes,' Bev replied.

Mr Jackson stood up.

'I am just going to get some coffee, would you like something to drink?'

'Yes please. I have some money.'

'Well then, shall we go and find the buffet car together?'

Bev followed him through the carriage and through the next one and the next one until they were in the buffet car. Mr Jackson ordered two cups of coffee and two packets of biscuits and Bev decided on a Coke and a bag of crisps. He was pleased that he had been allowed to pay for his own drink and he felt very grown-up as he returned to his carriage. The train was travelling very fast and it was difficult to walk straight as it rocked and lurched along. Whilst they ate and drank, Bev told them about Uncle Peter's boat.

'Canals, eh!' said Mr Jackson. 'I've read a few things about them but never been on one. The only canal I've seen is from this train, in fact if you come and sit over here you'll see it soon, the railway and canal are side by side for quite a stretch.'

Bev eagerly changed his seat and Mr Jackson continued.

'You could have seen it first when we left the station, but you would have to be quick — a brief glimpse of water and a couple of boats. They are always there, just a few yards outside Euston, must be near Camden Road I should think.'

A station flashed past before Bev could read its name, but Mrs Jackson knew it.

'Watford Junction,' she said. 'You'll soon see the canal now.'

And to Bev's delight there, just alongside the railway was a very narrow strip of water and there were a line of boats tied up. Some were painted in bright colours, green, red, blue, white — and there was something across the water further along, blocking the canal, but the train speeded on leaving the boats behind.

'That was a lock,' explained Mr Jackson. 'I expect you'll have a lot of those if you are going boating in the Midlands.'

'What is it for?' asked Bev.

'Well it's a way of getting boats up or down hills. I don't know exactly how they work, but you open the gates and put the boat inside and then either fill it up or let the water out until you are at the right level again. It looks hard work, but no doubt a strong lad like you will soon get the hang of it.'

The journey continued with Bev and Mr Jackson seeing just how often they could spot a canal. At Hemel Hempstead it could be seen from the station and what a lot of boats were tied up — and surely that was one inside a lock! At Berkhampstead the train slowed down for its first stop and here the canal had a boatyard — all the boats were painted in the same colours, red and white.

'They are for hire,' said Mrs Jackson. 'For people to have holidays on.'

'Are there boats for hire in Stoke?' asked Bev. 'If so I might find someone to play with.'

'I'm sure there are,' she replied.

And so the journey continued. Near Rugby they saw a marina. It looked as if hundreds of boats were moored there, and a little later the train, the canal and the M1 motorway were all side by side. It looked as if the boats on the canal were not moving at all but this was only because the cars were travelling so quickly. There were sudden glimpses of lock gates that stuck up out of woods or fields without any sign of water.

'Oh, it's there all right,' smiled Mr Jackson. 'Look over in the far corner of the field, there's a bridge, see it? The canal must turn and go in that direction.'

Bev saw a tiny red brick bridge but still no water — the canal was hidden in the depths of hedges and fields. He leant back and picked up a comic, he felt ready for it now, and he was very pleased that after all he had had company on his journey, as he had learnt something about canals, and it made his holiday sound even more exciting than ever.

There was a sudden roaring noise in Bev's ears and he felt himself being shaken.

'Come on, wake up, we're almost at Stoke.' He saw Mr Jackson standing over him.

'Well you have had a good nap; now you'll be all ready for those locks. Here we are.'

He placed Bev's holdall beside him and Bev, now thoroughly alert, stood looking out of the window as the train gave a final shudder and stopped.

'There's Aunt Jean,' he called out, and waved frantically.

Mr Jackson saw a very pretty young lady waving back as she ran up to the carriage. Bev rushed out to meet her.

'You've forgotten your comics!'

Mrs Jackson handed them out of the window, and Aunt Jean took them.

'Thank you for looking after me.'

He followed his aunt along the platform and out into the street.

'It's not far,' she said. 'But first of all I'll use this telephone to let your mother know you've arrived safely.'

Bev stood outside the telephone box, well, here he was at last, about to start a super holiday that he just knew was going to turn into an adventure.

CHAPTER TWO

Bev and Aunt Jean walked to the end of the street, turned right and crossed over a small hump-backed bridge — they were already at the canal — and there, tied up alongside the towpath, was the boat *Ratty*, named after Uncle Peter's favourite character from *Wind in the Willows*.

'Coo, what a long boat!'

'She's a full seventy-footer,' smiled Aunt Jean. 'You'll probably see one or two more like it, but not many. Most boats on the canals are between thirty and fifty-five feet.'

As they walked along the towpath Bev now saw that the gay colours and patterns which were painted on the sides were in fact pictures. Big bunches of fat roses, and there was a castle and —

'Welcome aboard!'

Uncle Peter poked his head out from a small entrance halfway along the boat. 'Here, give me your bag. Now mind the steps, they're a bit steep.'

The three wooden steps led down into a narrow passage with a door on each side. Bev followed his uncle into the compartment on the left and found himself in the galley. There was a gas stove with a refrigerator next to it, and opposite there stood a large sink and draining board; next there were shelves full of crockery and cupboards with sliding doors.

'Why it's got all the things we have at home!' he said.

A wooden partition with an opening on one side separated the galley from the next room.

'That's called a bulkhead,' explained his uncle as they now passed through into the cosy cabin next door. This was furnished with a big settee, a bench, two small armchairs... and the room seemed to go on and on....

'I'll take you right through the boat later and show you everything.'

Aunt Jean led him through the cabin and pointed to the doorway at the end.

'Leave your things in there and we'll have a cup of tea.'

Bev went into a tiny cabin which had a bunk bed, a chair and a small cupboard in the corner. A little round window was by the side of the bed. He put his blazer on the bed and went back into the other room where his aunt was setting out some delicious cakes on the table.

After tea Bev had his guided tour of *Ratty*. There were, he found, three ways to get into the boat. From the back where two doors led into the Art Gallery, and then from the front where you had to lift up a small wooden hatch on the roof before opening a door which took you directly into the snug cabin where Bev had left his things, and then of course there was the centre entrance, which Bev now saw had two very narrow doors and it also had a lift-up hatch.

'Now here at the back is where we sell our pictures and postcards,' explained Uncle Peter. Bev looked around at the colourful array hanging from both sides of the long narrow room. Pictures of boats, bridges, locks, people fishing — on a stand in the middle of the room postcards were displayed on racks and down at the end there was a counter covered with tea-towels which had canal pictures printed on them, and woolly hats, gloves and scarves which Aunt Jean knitted.

'And this is my studio.'

Uncle Peter went through the door at the end of the gallery and Bev followed him. Here there were jars of brushes, paints, stacks of canvasses, cardboard, paper — all a glorious jumble on a large bench that took up half the width and all the length of the room. A couple of high wooden stools were the only other furniture.

The room adjoining the studio was a bedroom and next to that a small compartment for the toilet and shower.

'I'll show you how they work later on. You have to be careful with water, not use too much. A boat has to find its own water and so we never wash our hands under a running tap for instance, in fact you must never leave a tap running.'

Bev didn't think this too much of a hardship. 'I'll only wash when I'm very dirty,' he said. 'That'll save water.'

'Oh no you won't!'

Aunt Jean had come through from the other end of the boat.

'You'll wash the same as you do at home, we've always enough water for that.'

Oh dear, thought Bev, but he noticed that Aunt Jean was smiling at him.

'Well, now you're back in our living quarters and it's time you unpacked. I'll show you where your clothes go.'

To Bev's delight, the tiny cabin with the bunk and little round window was to be his very own room. The bed lifted up to reveal storage for clothes and shoes, also extra blankets. The little cupboard had hooks and hangers.

'There's also a cupboard at the bottom of the stairs where you came in. That is where we keep our boating clothes, anoraks, over trousers and wellies.'

His aunt looked down at him.

'There are also a couple of lifejackets at the bottom of the cupboard — can you swim?' she asked.

Bev could, and he quickly showed his swimming trunks with two badges sewn on them.

'Oh that's all right then, afraid you won't be able to swim in the canal — but we'll probably find a river if it gets hot enough.'

Uncle Peter was still in the studio when Bev finished unpacking and he went in to see what he was doing.

'I'm getting my maps ready — come and have a look.'

Bev climbed on to the stool to see what was on the bench. Laid out in front of him was a large map but it was quite unlike any map that he had ever seen before. This one just had blue squiggly lines going up and down and across; some were thick lines, some thin, others dotted.

'Now we are here.'

His uncle pointed to a thin line going between the two names STONE and ETRURIA.

'This canal is the 'Trent and Mersey' and we are moored at Stoke-on-Trent which is very famous for pottery. Tomorrow we are going along here.' He followed the line with his pencil. 'Through these locks at Etruria and do you see this junction where another canal joins us? That is the Caldon Canal; we are going to travel all the way along it until we come to both ends.'

He laughed down at Bev's puzzled expression.

'Both?'

'It splits here, look, one channel goes to Leek and this one to Consall Forge.'

'Have you been there before?'

'Yes, but this time I want to stop for a while. There are some boats still using the canal for the original purpose it was built for, carrying pottery — and I am going to sketch them. I'd like to paint a few pictures of them later on.'

'What kind of boats are they?'

'Very much like ours, except they have no rooms for living in — all their space is for carrying the pots. You'll see hundreds of cups, saucers, oh, all kinds of things, all going along in a canal boat.'

'If we are going along the Caldon tomorrow, where will we go the next day?'

His uncle laughed out loud.

'Next day? Why it will take us about a week to travel the whole of the Caldon.'

Bev's eyes opened wide.

'But it's only a little line on the map.'

'You travel very slowly on a canal — there is a speed limit of four miles per hour.'

'*Four* miles per hour!'

Bev couldn't believe anything could go so slow.

'In fact we probably only do just over two and a half,' his uncle said. 'The canals are not very deep and special care must be taken not to damage the banks. If a boat goes fast then it makes a big wave behind it which hits the sides of the canal too hard and causes the bank to crumble and fall into the water.'

'And do we go through locks as well tomorrow?'

'Yes, that is the second reason that it takes up more time, but as far as we are concerned time doesn't matter.'

'Why not?'

'Well, we are lucky that we do not have to be anywhere by a certain time — that is, not usually. Sometimes of course we do have to keep on travelling to reach a particular town where we are taking part in a rally or festival. But usually we can just cruise when we feel like it. And this way is the best way to see and get to know all that's going on around you. Tomorrow we have to do some shopping in Hanley, so we will have an early breakfast and then we will be there by lunch time. I think that's enough canal talk for tonight. Time for bed.'

Bev lay on his bunk and snuggled into his sleeping bag. Through the little window he saw two stars move across the sky — to his surprise they stopped halfway across the window, and then moved backwards! They came into view slowly once again, stopped, then went back again. He sleepily realised that *Ratty* was gently rocking from side to side as his aunt and uncle moved at the other end of the boat, shutting up doors and windows for the night. The stars continued coming and going; but Bev no longer saw them — he was fast asleep.

CHAPTER THREE

After breakfast the next morning Bev watched his uncle check the engine then when all was ready he was shown how to untie the mooring ropes and coil them neatly on the front and back of the boat.

'You can come with me and see how the lock works, our first one is just past the bridge, so we'll walk along the towpath.'

'What about the boat?'

'Your aunt will steer *Ratty* — she always does, you see the locks are sometimes difficult, it's best for the men like us.'

Bev thought it must be difficult to steer *Ratty* and that Aunt Jean must be very clever to take such a long, long boat into such a small narrow lock.

'That's lucky,' said Uncle Peter as they reached the lock. 'It's ready for us.'

Bev looked at the edge of a deep chamber, with two narrow wooden gates at one end and one big one at the other. They had thick wooden beams sticking out and Uncle Peter crossed over the top of the gates, holding carefully on to the guard rails and then by leaning his back against the beam the gate swung slowly open. He then walked down the side of the lock, crossed over the top gate, and came back to open the other smaller gate.

Aunt Jean then very carefully brought the boat into the lock, and to Bev's surprise it *did* fit in — just. The nose of the boat touched the top gate and there was only a couple of feet between the back of the boat and the bottom gates.

Once the boat was safely inside and the gates closed behind it, Uncle Peter walked to the top end of the lock and using a curved iron thing he had been holding in his hand he started winding up a narrow iron ratchet fixed to a gate.

'This is a windlass,' he nodded to the curved iron tool. 'It is used to wind up the paddles — they are like big wooden doors which stop the water from coming into the lock. See how the water is rushing in now that I've lifted the paddle up a little way.'

Bev looked down into the lock to see *Ratty* beginning to rise up as a tremendous surge of water came swirling through the gates into the lock. Uncle Peter came across the lock and wound up the other paddle.

'Always remember to lift the paddles halfway at first, to allow the boat to rise steadily, and not get knocked about with too much water rushing in.'

As the boat rose steadily up and up the paddles were lifted to their maximum height and soon Aunt Jean was on the same level as Bev. When the water in the lock was at the same level as the canal, Uncle Peter leant on the balance beam of the gate and opened it and out sailed *Ratty*. The paddles were wound down, the gates closed and Bev and his uncle climbed on board.

'Can I have a go at the next lock please?'

'Yes, I'd be more than grateful for your help — we've another five before we stop for lunch and shopping.'

And so the morning passed, and Bev had quite a few surprises, for when he first leant against the gate nothing happened.

'You have to push hard,' grinned Uncle Peter. 'See these grooves on the ground made by a raised line of bricks? They're for putting your feet against to help you push — like this.'

He leant against Bev's gate as well, and copying his uncle Bev found that the gate slowly gave way and opened. When it came to winding up the paddles he just couldn't start his one at all.

'No, some of them are very stiff. I'll give it the first few turns, it will be a bit easier when the lock starts filling.'

His uncle came to his aid once again. To Bev's delight however he *could* unwind them, but even this was tricky and he found that you had to be careful in case the wedge slipped out of the racket, and then the paddle would drop down with a mighty splash and a tremendous bang.

'The spindles are worn in some places,' explained Uncle Peter. 'You have to remember that these locks were built over two hundred years ago, and many of them have not had as much maintenance done to them as they should — so always be careful when using a windlass on the winding gear. Never, never leave it on the spindle, as if the paddle should slip then the windlass would spin round so fast that it would fly off into the air — and it could cause a great deal of damage if it hit anyone.' He smiled down at Bev. 'And if it falls into the canal it is a pretty hopeless task to find it again.'

Bev listened carefully and as he slowly unwound the last paddle his uncle patted him on the shoulder.

'Well done! You've the makings of becoming a first class boatman.'

'Hey you two, are you coming aboard or not?'

It was Aunt Jean who had been patiently leaning on the tiller. *Ratty* had left the lock and was waiting for them alongside the towpath.

Bev stood by his aunt's side and watched the world slip slowly by.

'Did you notice the lock house?' she asked.

'Yes, it was a new one wasn't it? I thought it would be old.'

'Most of them are, but you see there has recently been a new road built right round the town and as the canal was by the side of it they had to take some of the land near the lock. So the towpath was moved and the canal altered slightly — and a new lock house had to be built.'

The next bridge they came to was very low and although the boat just scraped through, Aunt Jean had to duck her head as they went underneath. Bev noticed another lock in front and he called down into the boat, 'Lock ahead!'

Aunt Jean laughed as Uncle Peter emerged from the below: 'He's sounding like a real boater already.'

This lock was very very deep.

'I think it is the deepest on the system now, since it has been rebuilt,' his uncle told him. 'It is called "Etruria Lock".'

'That's a funny name,' said Bev.

'It is the name of this town. Josiah Wedgwood, the great pottery manufacturer, built a factory here in the eighteenth century and as the town grew up around it he named it Etruria, after an Italian town that was also famous for its pottery.'

'Do all the locks have names?'

'Most of them. They are numbered too.'

'That bridge had a number on it.'

'Yes — it helps you to find out where you are on the canal. If you drive a car you use a road map and look out for signposts. On the canal you use a waterways map and the bridge numbers are like the names on a road map. There are also signposts along the canal — you must look out for one. We'll look at a waterways map tonight and I'll explain how to read it. Now look in front of you, see just outside the lock we join another canal — that is the Caldon, where we are going.'

Before *Ratty* started along the Caldon they stopped to fill up with water and to empty the chemical toilet. A brick building by the side of the canal had the toilet facilities, and a water standpipe outside was conveniently placed for a hose to be fixed and to be run back to the boat.

'We carry about one hundred and ten gallons,' Uncle Peter said as he helped Bev unroll the hosepipe and insert it into a hole at the front of the boat. 'It will take a little while as this tap runs very slowly.'

Bev walked a little way along the towpath whilst waiting for the water tank to fill. The scenery so far had been factories, railways and large tracts of wasteland, not a bit like the country pictures of canals that his father had shown him... but he thought that now they had turned into the Caldon he could see in the distance green hills and trees.

'Hallo!'

Bev turned and saw a boy fishing from the bank. He had walked right past him and not noticed him, as he was sitting amongst some tall green and pink plants which hid him completely.

'You going up to Leek?' the young fisherman asked.

'Yes — well, I think that's the place, there are two ends to this canal aren't there?'

'Leek and Consall Forge — if you *are* going to Leek the fishing is smashing near the tunnel.'

'I don't know how to fish.'

'You've never fished!' He sounded shocked.

'No.'

'What do you do then — I mean when you're not at school?'

'I go out on my bike, or play in the park with my friends.'

'Don't they fish?' He sounded once more as if he had never heard of such an existence.

Before Bev could answer a shout went up: 'Hey Bev, we're ready.'

As he ran off Bev waved goodbye. The boy waved again and Bev thought that now it was him that looked longingly back to the boat.

The first two locks on the Caldon were yet another surprise for Bev — they were staircase locks which meant that when the boat rose up and left the first lock it went straight into a second lock. The top gate of the first became the bottom of the second.

As they rose up and up Bev looked at the cement factory alongside and the buildings behind.

'Not much scenery to boast about, is it?' said Uncle Peter. 'But that will soon change — we'll tie up outside Planet Lock, the next one and do our shopping and then after lunch you'll see some very pretty canal side — something I'm sure you will enjoy.'

CHAPTER FOUR

Bev helped Aunt Jean to wash up whilst Uncle Peter went into the gallery and prepared it for customers. They were going to moor just past the second bridge after the lock.

'Usually quite a few people there.' Aunt Jean stacked the plates on the shelf next to the sink. 'If the weather remains fine we'll stay until tomorrow.'

Bev looked disappointed.

'Cheer up, you'll find lots to do. One of the good things about a canal holiday is that you can have as much fun and find lots of interesting things in the places you pass through as you can on the boat. If you stay on the boat all the time you miss seeing the different villages, or playing in the woods. Sometimes when we stop in a very quiet place the birds and animals come very very close to the boat — you'll see.'

Uncle Peter started up the engine.

'You can help me steer, Bev. Look, I've put a box for you to stand on so that you can see over the top of the boat. Now, hold the tiller and keep it steady. The canal is pretty straight here and we're only going a short way. Now line up for the bridge ahead of you — like this.'

He put his hand over Bev's and gently swung the tiller

to the right. Bev saw that the front of *Ratty* turned to the left, the nose of the boat straightened up and they sailed through the bridge hole.

'Well done!'

His uncle smiled down at him and removed his hand so that Bev was left holding the tiller all on his own.

He thrilled to feel the vibration of the engine beneath him gently throbbing as if it was inside him. He looked along the top of the boat — what a long long boat it was. He felt as if he owned the world as he stood there steering this magnificent craft. He didn't dare move the tiller but clung to it fiercely.

'See the next bridge?' Uncle Peter clasped Bev's hand once again. 'We'll tie up just beyond it.'

Once the boat was safely moored, Aunt Jean took two cardboard posters and some string.

'Come and help me put these up.'

But Bev was staring round in surprise — whilst steering the boat he hadn't noticed that they had left behind the factories and wasteland.

Now they were surrounded by lawns, flower beds, and in front was a beautiful ornamental iron bridge on which a steady stream of people were crossing. Some of them stopped to look down at *Ratty*. A very imposing flight of stone steps led up to what looked like more gardens and tennis courts. They had moored in the middle of a park! But how could he get into it? There were railings on both sides of the canal which separated them.

Aunt Jean fixed one poster underneath the bridge and then walked back along the towpath to the next bridge and there was a small gate leading into the park. She fixed the second poster and Bev read:

VISIT *RATTY*
THE FLOATING
ART GALLERY
* * *
PICTURES
* * *
POSTCARDS
AND
CANALIA

and an arrow pointed towards the boat.

'If you want to go into the park this gate is the nearest to the swings,' said Aunt Jean. 'I think the best way to them is that direction, and over there is a lake —' she grinned '— if you're not fed up with water!'

'How long are we stopping here?' asked Bev.

'Oh we shall stay here until tomorrow — if it's nice and sunny then lots of people will take a walk through the park in the morning.'

'All right then.'

Bev ran off, turned and waved back.

'I'm making some tea about four o'clock,' his aunt called out.

He nodded and ran up the grassy bank and over the iron bridge. He too stopped and looked down at *Ratty* and felt very proud indeed to know that he was part of it. He could hear other people talking about the boat.

'She's a beauty, isn't she? Don't see many like her up here.'

'Nice life, I reckon that must be.'

Bev turned from the railings and soon found the playground. It was very much like the ones back home with swings, slides and see-saws. There were only a few very young children playing there and after a couple of goes on the swings he decided to inspect the rest of the park. He crossed over the velvety grass, and passed the tennis courts and bowling green and as he stood on top of that grand flight of steps he saw the lake twinkling in the sunshine. It was in the far corner of the park.

'I reckon I could reach that in about one minute if I ran fast,' he said.

'I could beat you!'

The voice came from behind. He turned and saw it was the boy who had been fishing.

'OK, you're on!'

They both took off and ran back over the bridge, scattering people in their path, on and on down the sloping grassy bank, along the curving pathway, both neck and neck, across the big circle of grass by the bandstand, and they finished up colliding together on the path encircling the lake, they fell, breathless, rolling about, until the boy sat up and laughed.

'That was a good race, we'll have another around the lake when you've got your breath back.'

Bev laughed as well and the rest of the afternoon he spent playing with his new friend Tom.

As they walked back to the boat Bev told Tom about Uncle Peter's boat but Tom cut in.

'I know all about it, my dad knows your uncle.'

'Does he? Is your father a painter?'

Tom laughed. 'Not in the same way as your uncle! No, my dad works for the B.W.B.'

'B.W.B?'

'That's who looks after all the canals — British Waterways Board. We live near the canal — if you come down to the tunnel you'll see our house.'

'What tunnel?'
'Harecastle Tunnel – we live almost on top of it.'
'Where is it?'
'Not far from here.'

They had now reached *Ratty* and Uncle Peter was still very busy with customers, but Aunt Jean invited Tom to have some tea with them. During tea she brought out a waterways map and Tom showed Bev where he lived.

'So you're Mr Langley's son?' said Aunt Jean.
'Yes.'
'We're coming along your way when we've been up to Leek and Consall.'
'Good, I'll tell Dad, he's found some old photos he wanted to show you.'

Uncle Peter now joined them.
'I've closed up for a break.'
He gratefully sat down with his tea.
'I thought I recognised you at the junction when you were fishing. Catch much?'
'No, so I decided to cycle along to the Park – glad I did, 'cos this is the first time I've been on a boat like this.'

Bev gasped. 'But you must have if you live near the canal!'

Tom laughed. 'Cost a packet to have a beauty like this,' he said. 'Anyway, I prefer to fish.' He stood up. 'I'll have to be getting back or Mum'll wonder what's happened. She's not too fond of water, always thinks I'll fall in and drown.'

'Can't you swim?' asked Bev.
'No,' said Tom. 'Never tried, don't fancy it.'
'I can swim,' Bev said proudly.
'Not in the canal you can't, it's not allowed!' Tom turned to Aunt Jean. 'Thank you for the tea.'

Bev waved to him as he walked down the towpath.
'Is it far to the tunnel?' he called out.
'No! I've left my bike with the park keeper.'
He ran across the bridge and waved goodbye again.

Later that evening, Uncle Peter gave Bev a notebook. On the cover he had drawn a picture of *Ratty* and along the top were the words BEV'S LOG BOOK.

'Do you know what a log book is?'

'Yes, captains of ships write in what happens every day.'

'Not only captains, all good boaters use them. I write in mine every day, I find it a good check on where we've been, how much diesel or gas we use and lots of other details. I thought you might like to write about what you've done and seen each day.'

'That's a good idea! Perhaps I could draw some pictures, too,' he asked. 'I'm much better at drawing than writing.'

'Well, why not do a bit of both, write at the top of the page and draw a picture at the bottom.'

Bev took his log book into his cabin, and that night he sat up in bed, knees drawn up and he wrote down about the locks, how he had steered *Ratty*, and best of all how he had met Tom. He drew a picture of Tom fishing, hidden amongst the grass and bushes. He was almost asleep when an angry squawking sound right outside his window made him jump up in alarm. He peered out and just below him disappearing into the weeds by the bank was a little black duck with a black and white fan-shaped tail. What a lot of noise from such a little thing! Was it a duck? He settled back into his sleeping bag telling himself that he must ask Aunt Jean tomorrow.

CHAPTER FIVE

The Caldon Canal twisted and turned, went under very low bridges, and once Bev helped Uncle Peter with a bridge that had to be raised by pulling on a chain.

'Lift bridges come in all shapes and sizes, all over the canal system,' Uncle Peter said, as he heaved and tugged the chain whilst Aunt Jean steered the boat through the very narrow gap.

Almost as soon as they left Hanley Park they were enclosed by the pottery buildings. As it was Sunday no one was working in them, but Bev saw stacked near the windows hundreds of white jugs, cups, and saucers; and in one room there were dozens of large white china dogs all standing together on a bench. Some had black spots painted on them and others awaited their turn.

As they emerged from a very low bridge that made the canal quite dark, the boat turned a sharp bend and, standing beside the canal, was a very funny-shaped chimney.

'That is a bottle kiln — it's shaped like a big bottle made of bricks,' explained his uncle. 'It is a furnace where they baked all the pots. There must have been hundreds of them years ago, but they are no longer in use — too old-fashioned and slow for modern potteries. Still, it is nice a few of them have been left for us to see.'

Soon after this they passed a boat moored at the back of one of the potteries. It was nearly as long as *Ratty* but very different. It was all open with no roof or sides.

'That is for carrying the pots from this factory to their Packing Department, about four miles along the canal. I want to make some pictures of it loaded — we'll stop on the way back,' said Uncle Peter.

The countryside gradually came back to the canal with vast open stretches of fields, hills, woods... and then, Bev saw for the first time a boat moving towards them. It was shorter than theirs but painted in bright colours, green and red with a blue and yellow diamond pattern on the front. The man steering waved as they passed and Bev and Uncle Peter waved back.

'Is that a holiday boat?' asked Bev.

'No, that was a private one. We shall start seeing the holiday boats soon. They start out late on Saturday afternoons, and as there are no boatyards between Stoke and here we haven't met up with any. But we will.' He grinned. 'Aunt Jean will probably have a moan about it, she likes to have the canal to herself.'

'There doesn't seem much room on this canal for many boats, we only just managed to pass that one.'

'Oh, we can pass each other — it is when someone new to the canal tries to overtake us — they don't realise it is too shallow and you cannot go fast so one of us usually gets stuck on the side and that is when your aunt gets cross.'

'How do you get off again?'

'Oh, it's not too bad, if it happens you'll see what we do.'

There were more locks ahead, and this time Bev found that he and Uncle Peter had worked out a routine between them and they quickly and quietly worked *Ratty* through them. Later in the afternoon they reached the section where the canal divided into two. To Bev's delight they were going along the part that carried the canal high over the top of the lower section. They went through some more locks and then were sailing high up in the air in a trough of water held in a beautiful ornate bridge.

'This is called an aqueduct,' his aunt told him. Bev peered down and across the fields.

'Look!' he cried, and pointed to patches of blue and white that were moving in between the trees. 'What's that?'

His aunt laughed.

'It's a boat on the other section. You can't see the canal because the bushes are so thick — it looks as if the boat is moving across the fields, doesn't it?'

Ratty now took them through a beautifully wooded part of the Caldon Canal. There were swans, ducks — and Bev saw again that funny little black duck with the fan-shaped tail. Aunt Jean, sitting at the front of the boat, told him it was a moorhen.

'There are hundreds of them, they are everywhere on the canals. You can always recognise them because they have such gaudy colours on the beaks and heads. It's like a red shield on the forehead that extends down to the beak, which has a yellow tip. If you see them out of the water, they run very fast on thin greeny-yellow legs.'

The canal now became very wide and resembled a lake; and suddenly in front of them was a tunnel.

'We shall stay here tonight,' said Aunt Jean.

'Are we going through the tunnel?' asked Bev.

'No, we are too long — we have to turn around this side of it, there is no room at the other end.'

Bev was disappointed until his aunt reminded him that they would be going through Tom's tunnel in a few days and that was a *very* big tunnel — you couldn't see through it to the other end like you could this one.

'Tom said the fishing was good here,' said Bev.

'I don't fish, I'm afraid,' Uncle Peter shook his head.

'I'd like to try and catch one,' Bev said.

'Well, when we go into Leek you can buy a fishing net,' his aunt told him.

Once *Ratty* was safely moored for the night Uncle Peter started to work on some pictures and Aunt Jean took Bev for a walk. They went up to the tunnel and Bev peered through to see the hole of daylight at the other end. As they turned away a man with a fishing rod and a large bag came across the field towards them.

'Are you going to fish?' Bev called out to him.

He look startled and it was obvious that he had not noticed them.

'Oh, er, yes — yes I am,' he mumbled.

'It's very good here, isn't it?' asked Bev.

The man turned away.

'So I've been told.'

He walked to the edge of the canal, and Aunt Jean took hold of Bev's hand and pulled him away.

'Come on, Bev, you can help me do some vegetables for dinner tonight.'

Bev would much rather have stayed and watched the fisherman, but as they crossed over the fields towards their boat his aunt explained that sometimes fishermen were very upset if people talked to them when they were fishing.

'He's probably very fussy about the exact spot he uses and he doesn't want us to hang around watching him. Never mind, you'll see lots of other fishermen.'

As they returned to the boat the man started to take his rod out and walk towards the tunnel.

CHAPTER SIX

Before returning down the canal, Aunt Jean and Bev did some shopping in Leek. There was a market and on one of the stalls Bev bought a bright yellow fishing net. When they tied up for the evening he sat on the bank and with one of his aunt's plastic containers filled with canal water by his side, he started to fish. To his delight three tiny grey speckled fish soon swam into his net and he quickly turned them out into the container. But half an hour later when it was time for him to have his evening meal, he still only had those three fish.

'I think that's pretty good for your first effort,' said Uncle Peter. 'I see fishermen on the bank for hours and they never seem to catch anything — you have to have a lot of patience to be a fisherman.'

After their meal all three went for a walk across the fields to see where the water came from that fed the canal — it was a large lake, Rudyard Lake, and here there were a great many fishermen. On the way back to the boat, Aunt Jean said, 'That was an angling contest to see who could catch the most fish, or perhaps the biggest.'

'Tom said the fishing was good near the tunnel, perhaps he meant this place,' said Bev.

'I expect he knows all the best places,' replied Aunt Jean. 'We'll have to get his advice when we see him.'

The next day they reached Hazlehurst Junction again, and this time they went underneath the aqueduct. As they came through the archway, Uncle Peter pointed up and Bev saw another boat above them!

That night they tied up at Cheddleton, and the next morning Uncle Peter took Bev to see a watermill which was still working. The huge mill stones ground flint into fine powder and this was used in the making of pottery.

The canal next day entered once again into deep woodland, and to Bev's delight they moored near another boat. As he sat on the bank with his fishing net, a girl with a dog jumped off the boat and came over to him.

'Hallo, caught anything?'

'No.'

'Do you live on the boat?'

She sounded envious.

'Yes, it belongs to my aunt and uncle — I'm only with them for a month.'

'Lucky you, we've only got ours for a week.' She smiled at him shyly. 'Would your uncle let me have a look at some pictures? I want to buy a present for my grandmother.'

Bev took her back to *Ratty* and helped her choose a small black and white sketch of two boats carrying coal. While they were looking round the gallery she told him her name was Judy, and that she was pleased to see Bev as she was the only child on their boat. Her sister had hurt her ankle playing netball, and it was still in plaster, so she had gone to stay with her grandmother.

Judy's parents came to see the art gallery as well, and the two children and Prince, the dog, went off for a walk whilst the grown-ups talked about the pictures. The canal was very beautiful here, with trees clinging to the steep sides of the woods that rose up from the banks.

'Super for hide and seek!' said Bev, and soon they were climbing up and up, deeper into the woods; and Judy, who was the first to hide, found the big trees easy to climb and she sat on a big branch just above Bev's head whilst he searched for her. Bev too found lots of good hiding places, and the game went on for at least four turns each. Then Judy picked up a long piece of wood.

'This could be a super sword, let's play Robin Hood!'

'He used a bow and arrow,' said Bev.

'And swords. I saw a picture of him fighting the Sheriff of Nottingham.'

'All right, wait till I find one.'

'You can have this. I'm Maid Marion, she didn't use a sword.'

The woods were once again the ideal place for Robin Hood, with lots of bushes to take cover in, trees to climb as a look-out, and Prince became Maid Marion's guard dog.

A shout from down below near the canal brought the children back to reality. It was Uncle Peter calling them. They scrambled down the banks and to their great surprise found that Judy's parents were going to have their meal on board *Ratty*.

'Oh super!' shouted Judy.

During the evening Uncle Peter told lots of stories about the other canals. He and Aunt Jean had travelled on all of them.

'I envy your way of life very much,' said Judy's father. 'A world so different from the rush and tear of motor cars and telephones.'

'Can we live on a narrowboat?' asked Judy.

'I'm afraid we can't. There are no canals near my office, and unlike Peter I would not be able to carry my work around with me.'

Judy and her parents were cruising the Caldon Canal the opposite way to *Ratty*. They were now on their way back to the junction to go along the section to Leek.

'Perhaps we'll meet up later in the week,' said Bev.

'It will have to be on the Caldon, because we are going down to Stone to return our boat, and you are going through Harecastle Tunnel, aren't you?' Judy's father said.

'I'm sure we'll see you somewhere on the Caldon,' Aunt Jean said. 'We shall be mooring near Hanley Park for a day at least, Peter wants to sketch the pottery boat.'

'Oh good,' Bev looked at Judy. 'We can play in the Park — I know it pretty well, I've been there before,' he boasted, whilst the grown-ups went on to discuss the approximate day when they would meet again.

Very early next morning whilst Bev was still in bed he heard the chug-chug-chug of a boat, and felt *Ratty* moving gently backwards and forwards. From his window he saw Judy's dad at the tiller of their boat. Prince was by his side — they were off already.

He waved and opened the window.

'Bye, see you at Hanley!'

Prince barked back and Judy waved from a window at the front of the boat.

Ratty continued down the canal until they reached Consall, and here the canal was unnavigable. They turned around and spent the day cruising back the way they had come.

'It's amazing how different the canal scenery looks when you travel the opposite way,' said Aunt Jean.

And she was right. Bev noticed a house perched high on

the banks that had been hidden when they were coming down the canal — and on this journey, they met a lot more holiday boats. Almost at every lock there was a boat, and quite often people came up for a chat, and Bev met many other children, and Uncle Peter sold quite a few things, not only pictures but postcards and tea-towels as well. In fact so many times did they stop that they took an extra day travelling back along this section of the canal, but it didn't matter — Bev was finding out that when boating on a canal, time wasn't important at all.

Once more they travelled beneath the aqueduct at the junction, and then they were passing the funny bottle kilns again. This time the people were working in the potteries, and they waved from their workshops, and Bev now saw the black spots being painted onto the dogs, and he saw too that the pottery boat was working as well. It passed them filled with small white basins and jugs — they were stacked in plastic baskets, without any wrapping paper or straw.

'Don't need it,' explained Uncle Peter. 'At their speed the movement of the boat is very slight and gentle. They only have to travel four miles and no locks. It is nice to see the canal being used for its original purpose, the very reason Josiah Wedgwood helped to finance the building of canals.'

They moored outside the Park once again, and Uncle Peter took a small folding-up stool and walked back to draw the pottery and the boat.

Bev and Aunt Jean did some shopping in a little side street near the Park and Bev spent the next day fishing and playing on the swings.

The following afternoon Judy's boat came down the canal and tied up behind *Ratty*. This time Judy's parents insisted that the evening meal was to be on their boat.

'Not quite so comfy as *Ratty*,' said Judy's mother.

'I think it's smashing!' Bev was looking around the boat which was divided into smaller cabins in order to accommodate all four people.

'Of course, you've not been on a holiday boat have you?' said Aunt Jean.

'I'll show you round,' offered Judy, and the two children went to explore the rest of the boat.

Bev was very impressed with the way an extra bunk could be raised up from the side of a small cabin.

'I've got this to myself,' explained Judy. So we don't need to have it fixed up — it would have been if my sister had come with us.'

'I've a cabin to myself too,' Bev told her.

The galley was very much like *Ratty*'s but the dining area was smaller.

'That's because our boat is open-planned.' Uncle Peter had joined the children. 'Holiday boats are made in compartments, so that everyone can have a separate sleeping compartment — see, when this dining table is lowered it rests on these ledges, then the cushions slide across and become mattresses, and lo and behold, you have a double bed for the night.'

As he spoke, Uncle Peter folded up the legs beneath the table, and lowered it on to the ledges sticking out from the seats on either side of the table.

'That's where we sleep.' Judy's father was standing behind Bev. 'But if you want any dinner tonight, I think we'd better get the table up again, or else the cook might get angry at spoiling her meal.'

Both families enjoyed their evening meal together, and Bev felt sad at the thought of saying goodbye to Judy the next morning.

'I expect you'll soon meet another holiday boat — there are lots of them out now,' said Judy. 'It's me that should feel sad — I'm having to go back home after only a week on a canal boat — not like lucky old you having a whole month!'

As Judy's boat had to be back at Stone by first thing Saturday they said goodbye very early next morning, and Bev decided to have another go at fishing.

This time he caught a tiny grey fish that had some small red spots on its side, and then a very fat fish swam into his net. He quickly turned them out into his plastic container and ran to show his aunt.

'They are sticklebacks,' she told him. 'Keep them in the container for a little while only — they will have to be put back into the canal because that box isn't really big enough for them, and of course they won't be able to find any food in it.'

Bev took his box back, and sat down to fish again. Every now and then he looked at his fish swimming happily around but suddenly the fat one tried to bite the red speckled one.

'Oh dear,' said Bev.

'What's the matter?'

It was Uncle Peter who had returned from his sketching. He looked into Bev's plastic box.

'I think it's time to return them to their home, don't you?' And as Bev sadly tipped them back into the canal his uncle said, 'And it's time we went to find that tunnel. Come on Bev, it's your turn to steer again.'

This time Uncle Peter allowed Bev to hold the tiller and guide the boat without any help. Bev soon found out how quick he had to be to push or pull the tiller over in order to avoid going into the bank, and he felt very grown-up when he actually steered *Ratty* into a lock! He only scraped the boat against the gates a little bit, as it slid into the narrow opening.

'Well done!' Aunt Jean was standing by his side. 'Don't worry about that little knock. Canal boats are built to withstand a few like that — you've done very well!'

When they reached the junction where the Trent and Mersey Canal joined the Caldon, they turned right. Now they were in the middle of factories, railways and towns once again, and in fact within a very short while the canal actually went right through a steelworks.

The canal was roofed over, making it seem like night-time. Only a few dim lights could be seen hanging from beams in long dark sheds, and there was one bare yellow lamp shining through the dusty windows of a little wooden office. Two empty boats were tied to a wharf.

'Not much going on here, now,' Uncle Peter sounded sad. 'I expect it will all be closed up soon.'

'Why?' asked Bev.

'Things have changed in the making of steel and now these works are out of date — like the bottle kilns you saw.'

About four miles further on, the canal had open grassy wasteland as scenery, and all along the banks, almost to the entrance of the tunnel, there were fishermen.

Bev looked for Tom, but he wasn't there.

'I expect we'll see him later on — we have to tie up here for the night, because the tunnel is closed for us until tomorrow morning,' said his uncle.

He explained that there was only room inside the tunnel for boats to travel one way at a time. Boats going north to south went in the afternoon, and those going south to north, like *Ratty*, would be able to travel in the morning, after ten o'clock.

'Once we're moored up for the night, I'll take you to the tunnel-keeper's house, that is where Tom lives. I've had my post sent on to there, so we'll collect it, and perhaps Tom will be home, and you can play with him.'

CHAPTER SEVEN

Harecastle Hill had not one tunnel going through it but three — Tom told Bev about them as they walked along the path that led from his house perched on the side of the hill down to the mouth of the two canal tunnels.

'There are two canal tunnels, and one railway tunnel. The first canal one was dug over two hundred years ago, here it is, it's not used now.'

Bev stood at the edge of the water which was almost covered with weeds — a small brick archway leading into a dark interior was all that he could see.

'There was no towpath inside,' Tom continued. 'So the boatman had to push their boats through by lying on planks of wood which were placed across the boats and they pushed their feet against the wall. Sometimes they lay on the cabin and pushed against the roof of the tunnel. Leggers, they were called.'

'I thought you said last night that horses had pulled the boats in the old days,' said Bev.

'So they did, but as there was no towpath they had to leave the horses outside the tunnel — they were walked over the top and met the boats at the other end.'

'How long is the tunnel?'

'Nearly two miles — it took so long to get a boat through that there were traffic jams.'

'Fancy having traffic jams two hundred years ago!'

'My dad's got some pictures showing all the boats queuing up — I'll show you when we get back home.'

'When did they build the second tunnel?'

'About fifty years later — that one had a towpath, so the horses could pull the boats through, and that made it easier and quicker. Look, here it is.'

'The boys had now walked over the top of the entrance of the first tunnel and down the side of it to come to the mouth of the second tunnel. This tunnel had a striped bar hanging across the opening.

'What's that for?' asked Bev.

'Well, the tunnel is very old, and parts of it have dropped, because of subsidence from the coal mines —'

'Sub what?' interrupted Bev.

'Subsidence,' repeated Tom. 'When coal is taken out of the mines, the earth all around it gets loose and it drops into holes and things — and some buildings and this tunnel drop as well.'

'I know,' said Bev. 'It's like when you dig sandcastles, if you're not careful, the outside walls fall down while you're scooping out sand from the middle.'

'Well, I don't know if it's the same thing. My dad'll tell you more about it — anyway, this tunnel had dropped a bit and the roof is very low in places, so all boats are measured before being allowed in.'

'And that bar is a test for them — they have to get under it,' said Bev.

'That's right — it's called a gauge — oh come on, I don't want to stand here all day.'

Tom walked away, over the top of the tunnel. 'I'll take

you over the top and show you where me and my friends play.'

'OK,' said Bev. 'You know, you are lucky, Tom, living on top of a tunnel and right beside a canal.'

But Tom wasn't listening. He had run off and was disappearing into the scrubby woods. Bev chased after him, he didn't want to be here by himself as he found the dark tunnels very eerie.

It wasn't long before they met up with two of Tom's friends, Mike and Terry, and they decided to play together. Mike was mad about science fiction, and so they all became astronauts exploring a new planet. The ground around them did in fact resemble a moonscape.... in the far distance were the chimneys and bottle kilns of the potteries, and leading up to the tunnel the vast open wasteland of derelict buildings, wharves and quarries, and the sides and top of the tunnel a mixture of scrubby grass and brambles, with vast tangles of hawthorn bushes. Bev and Tom went poking around on the far side of the hill, and with sticks as Geiger counters they searched for hidden treasures.

Suddenly Bev cried out. 'Tom! Tom, look what I've found!'

They were almost at the bottom of the other side of the hill, near the tunnel entrance, and Bev was pointing to a wooden box that was partially covered with soil and leaves, underneath a bush.

The four boys stood looking at it.

'Don't touch it,' said Tom.

'Wonder what's inside?' asked Terry.

'I'll go down to the tunnel office, there's a phone there, and I'll ring dad.' Tom ran off whilst the others kept guard.

After a few minutes, Tom came panting back.

'It's locked up, didn't realise it was so late. Never mind, we'll just leave it here and go back home and dad'll come out and see to it.'

'Will it be all right to leave it?' asked Bev.

'No one ever comes up here — only us,' said Mike. 'Let's chuck some more dirt on it, just to make sure.'

And he scooped some up and threw it onto the top of the box. The others helped him, and soon the box was securely hidden from view.

Mr Langley and Uncle Peter were sorting through old pictures of the canal when the boys returned.

'Look, Bev, this is what the canal was like a hundred years ago, see all those boats carrying coal?'

But the boys were too excited by their find, and they all started talking at once.

'We've found a box.'

'Guess what's hidden on the other side of the tunnel?'

'I think there's a bomb.'

Mr Langley had to raise his voice. 'Hold on, hold on, goodness, what a noise! Now sit down, all of you, that's right. Now then, Tom, what's all this about?'

Tom explained how they had been playing amongst the bushes on the hill, and they had discovered a box half hidden underneath one of them.

'What kind of box?' asked his father.

'A big wooden one,' said Tom.

Mr Langley looked thoughtful.

'Hmm! I wonder....' he said. 'Where is it now?'

He sounded very interested, and the boys became excited and started talking all at once again —

'Do you know what it is?'

'Is it a body?'

Mr Langley went across the room and picked up the telephone. He turned to Tom.

'What did you do with it — you didn't touch it, did you?'

'No,' said his son. 'We've buried it. It was too big for us to move anyway.'

Uncle Peter looked enquiringly at Mr Langley, as he dialled a number.

'Hallo, this is Mr Langley, tunnel keeper at Harecastle — oh it's you, Jack, that's good. I wonder if you could come over, yes, now. I think my boy has found something you're looking for. Yes — OK. Right, about a quarter of an hour. Goodbye.'

Bev couldn't sit still, he rushed up to Mr Langley.

'It's buried treasure, isn't it? I found buried treasure!'

Mr Langley smiled. 'Well, we don't know for sure what it is, do we — but I'll tell you what it might be.'

He explained that last week the police had told him there had been a burglary in a large house near Kidsgrove. It was the fourth break-in that month in that area. Someone had seen a car parked near the top of the tunnel very late one night, but nothing else had given any lead to the thieves. None of the stolen goods had been recovered, so it looked as if they were being hidden for a while, until perhaps the right buyer could be found.

'What was stolen — jewels, gold?' asked Bev.

'Mostly silver, gold ornaments and some jewellery.'

When Sergeant Dallow arrived he wasted no time and soon the four boys and the three men were climbing up the hill and over the top of the tunnel to the other side. Bev ran ahead — he knew exactly where his treasure lay.

Picking up a big stick, he poked the ground beneath the hawthorn bush.

'Hold on, sonny.'

It was the sergeant, slightly out of breath in keeping up with the children. He took the stick from Bev and stood looking at the ground. The soil was crumbly and loose all around the base of the bush.

'We're too late,' he said. 'No, don't touch anything,' he warned the boys. 'I'll get a couple of men with the dogs to have a look around.'

'But —' started Bev.

'Sorry to disappoint you,' said the sergeant. 'But it's been a great help to us — you've done a good day's work. Now I'd better get my men here, it's getting dark already, and I'd like to get a search started before it gets too murky up here.'

Later that evening Bev and Tom sat in Tom's bedroom. From the window they could look down on to the canal. It was very still and dark with only the lights from the boats that were moored up outside the tunnel, reflecting on the water.

Both the boys were disappointed that they hadn't recovered the stolen property.

'Never mind, we nearly did,' said Tom. 'It was a good game anyway.'

'Wish I could stay and play with your friends again,' said Bev.

'Well, you're going through the tunnel tomorrow — that's smashing!' said Tom.

'Have you been inside?' asked Bev.

'Only once. Dad took me through on a working boat — it's ever so dark and eerie in there.'

'Were you frightened?'

'No, of course not….' Tom stopped and after a pause said quietly, 'But there are ghosts in there.'

'Ghosts!' Bev jumped.

But before Tom could explain, Aunt Jean's voice called out, 'Hey, you two, supper's ready.'

A few minutes later the two boys, Mr and Mrs Langley, and Uncle Peter and Aunt Jean were all sitting round the big wooden table in the kitchen.

'Dad, tell Bev about the Harecastle ghost,' said Tom.

'Oh yes, you must look out for her tomorrow.'

'Her!' Bev was surprised. 'Is it a she ghost?'

'Well, it's like this.' Mr Langley sat back in his chair. 'There was a husband and wife who worked a pair of boats on a regular run from Middlewich down to Burton-on-Trent — mainly salt they carried. Now there's a lot of locking on that run, especially between Kidsgrove and Harecastle, Heartbreak Hill the boatmen called that stretch. Well, on one of their journeys, this couple had been held up in a traffic jam as one of the locks was not in use. Now time was money, if you didn't get your cargo to its destination quickly, you might miss getting another load for your return journey. The husband told his wife that they would not have time to stop for breakfast, she would have to cook it whilst they went through the tunnel.

She did not agree, and they had a row, but of course as she had to steer the butty boat behind her husband and help with the locking there was little she could do. By the time they reached the tunnel they were both very hungry and in a bad temper. Once inside the tunnel the wife went down into the cabin, but half an hour later she had not produced any breakfast. Her husband left his own boat and went back to see what was wrong — she was sitting down by the stove doing nothing at all. He shouted at her and they had an argument, she ran up on deck, he followed, they struggled together and she fell over the side into the cold black water. The horse had all this time continued to tow the boats, so the boats had moved some distance away from the accident. The poor man walked back along the dark towpath with a lamp, but never found his wife. Since that day many boaters have heard screams and cries. They always come from the same part of the tunnel, and the water often splashes violently as well, against the opposite side to the towpath.'

Bev listened with a mixture of fear and excitement.

'Is she always there?'

'Oh no, but you never know when she will come back — she's looking for her boat, you see — if she's in a good mood, you might smell bacon and eggs frying — I reckon she's sorry she didn't cook that breakfast.'

Mr Langley started eating his supper again.

'Come on, Bev, eat up.... You'd better have something inside you, just in case you do meet up with Kit Cluckbucket.'

'That's a funny name.'

'It's a very old name in these parts, you'll still find a few of them around today,' said Uncle Peter.

'Anyway' — it was Aunt Jean reminding her busband — 'I'm afraid, Bev, that you won't be going through the tunnel tomorrow — you'll have to wait a couple of days.'

'Of course, I'd almost forgotten, what with exciting news of buried treasure and burglars.' Uncle Peter turned to Bev. 'I've just sorted through my post and I have to go to London for a few days. A chance to talk about an exhibition of my pictures has come along and —'

'Are we going to London then instead?' Bev sounded disappointed.

'*You're* not!' laughed his Aunt Jean. 'Uncle Peter and I

are going by train — it would take too long to go by *Ratty*, we have to be there quicker than that — and you are staying here with Tom, and —'

But Bev heard nothing more — he was going to live in the tunnel house! Sleep in that room on top of the tunnel — and with Tom!

CHAPTER EIGHT

The next morning *Ratty* was locked up and moored alongside the towpath near to the tunnel keeper's office, and Bev moved into the tunnel house. Mr Langley drove Uncle Peter and Aunt Jean to the railway station, and the two boys planned their day.

'Why don't you go boating? After all, Bev is on a boating holiday,' said Tom's mother.

'I thought you said you hadn't got a boat?' Bev turned to Tom.

'It's not a canal boat. I had an inflatable one for my birthday.'

'Would you like me to make up a picnic?' asked Mrs Langley.

Both boys thought that a good idea.

'We'll take the binoculars and do some bird watching as well.'

Tom rushed upstairs to get them, and Bev helped pack their lunch.

Half an hour later Tom's boat was ready and the sandwiches and drinks were stowed beneath a seat. Tom showed Bev how to put on a lifejacket.

'But I can swim!' Bev protested.

Mr Langley, who had by now returned from the station, insisted on both boys wearing one.

'Better safe than sorry,' he said. 'If you capsize near a lock, the current can be very fierce. Now let me see if you have tied it correctly — make sure it's comfortable,' and he thoroughly checked both boys before allowing them to start.

Tom took the oars and off they went, back along the canal to Tunstall.

Bev found it very different from travelling in *Ratty* — now he was so close to the water, and he could see what a strange colour it was. When he looked down into it, the browny liquid had orangey glints in it, and yet when Tom dipped his oars into it, the water running of them was a phosphorescent green.

'It's the iron in the soil,' explained Tom 'On the other side of the tunnel the water is a light orange colour — like tomato soup — didn t you notice it?'

He rowed very well, and Bev hoped he would let him have a go soon.

'We'll stop after the next bridge,' Tom said. 'There's a bit of open ground not far away, we might see some birds there.'

Bev thought there were too many buildings around. They were now in between the towns of Tunstall and Longport, and factories and old buildings, along with the ruins of wharves, warehouses and sheds, stood all around.

However, to Bev's surprise, the birds did in fact inhabit quite a lot of places — he soon picked out a nest built of grass and twigs, which was perched on a ledge of broken bricks — it was quite open for all to see, and the young hedge sparrows were cheeping and shrieking for more from their parents.

'I wonder why they made a nest there?' asked Bev. 'If they are hedge sparrows, why didn't they find a hedge, there are some further along the canal?'

'Perhaps they found a good supply of food nearby,' Tom explained. 'See all those bits of bread lying over there — I bet some of the men in the factory come out and have their dinner-hour by the canal, and they feed the birds.'

Just as the boys were about to start off in the boat once more, Tom spied a funny round ball of grass and moss. It seemed to be hanging from a straggly bush that was almost hidden in the tall grass growing against a broken-down tin fence.

'That's a long-tailed tit's nest.' He pointed it out to Bev. 'I'll come back later in the year, and if it's empty by then I'll take it to school for our nature table.'

The boys waited to see if any birds were actually in the nest, but no activity could be seen, and they quietly left and rowed back along the canal.

The day sped by so quickly. Bev had a go at rowing, and found it was much harder to keep the boat travelling in a straight line than he thought. Tom made it look so easy.

'You'll soon learn. I was like you when I started,' encouraged Tom.

They had their picnic outside an old flint mill. It was now being rebuilt as a museum. The workmen who were putting the roof on had stopped for their lunch, and they helped the boys tie up the boat and after they had eaten their sandwiches they showed them around the building. The original chimney was still standing and it even had its name in white letters running down the side of it.

'I bet this was a busy wharf,' said Tom. 'Just think how many potteries they supplied with flint from here.'

One of the workmen told them that his grandfather had worked on the boats.

'It wasn't only flint they carried. My old grandad had clay, bricks and even Guinness as cargo.'

They rowed back home very slowly. Some holiday boats passed them, and they watched a fisherman for a while and although Tom envied him his rod, he didn't catch anything, and so they moved on.

As they approached the tunnel, Bev, who was looking through the binoculars said, 'I can see that man who was fishing at the other tunnel.'

'What man?' asked Tom.

'Oh, I forgot, I was with Auntie Jean,' Bev explained. 'He seemed very cross to see us, and walked away to the tunnel with his rod.'

'It was probably his favourite spot,' said Tom. 'He didn't want strangers around making a noise and upsetting the fish — now come on, your turn to row, just a good few pulls and we're home.'

CHAPTER NINE

'You're not bad at drawing, but it's easy to see you don't know anything about fishing.'

Tom was watching Bev finish off a sketch in his log-book.

It had been raining ever since the boys awoke, and they had spent the day reading and playing games indoors.

'What do you mean?' asked Bev.

'Well, that fisherman hasn't got the right things with him, only a rod.'

'That's all he had.'

'What's he going to sit on, where's his bait, what does he carry the bait in, and where's his keepnet?'

'Keepnet?'

'A folding-up net to put your catch in. With that super rod he would just have to have all the other bits and pieces. And if he's walked all that way along the towpath to that spot, he'll want to sit down. He must have had a basket around, and you didn't see it.'

'No, he only stood with the rod, and he had that big bag lying by his side, see I've put it in, it's there.'

Bev pointed with his pencil to a large square he had drawn against the man's leg.

'Well, I don't know what that is, but it's not for bait or nets.'

'Perhaps he had just finished, and had packed everything away, because when I saw him through the binoculars —' Bev suddenly stopped. 'That's funny, when we reached the tunnel he had gone, and yet he didn't pass us walking back along the towpath. He must have gone up the hill and over the tunnel.'

'Then he had a jolly long walk to the road. Did you say it was the same man you saw outside Leek Tunnel?'

'Yes.'

'Then he must be on holiday and trying out different places. He can't be a member of our local angling society. Wonder if he had a ticket to fish here today. I'll ask dad later, he's the water bailiff for this stretch.'

The rain stopped at last and the boys went out to find Mike and Terry, there was just time for a quick game of football in the park at Kidsgrove.

When they reached the park, however, they found that the grass was too wet for playing on.

'I know,' said Tom. 'Let's go and see the boats going through the tunnel — it'll be the last lot through tonight.'

'Yes,' said Terry. 'And we can race them and meet them coming out the other side.'

There were three boats just entering the tunnel from the Kidsgrove end, all holiday boats. A canoe was tied up outside with no one in it.

'That one won't be going,' explained Tom, and he pointed to a notice nailed outside the tunnel:

UNPOWERED BOATS
NOT ALLOWED
INSIDE

'Too dangerous, it's a long tunnel, and very dark in there. You only have the light from the front of your own boat.'

The boys started off as soon as the boat entered the tunnel and what a race they had! Tom was out in front, with Mike and Terry close on his heels. Bev, not knowing the way, lost sight of them and had to call out. They waited for him to catch up.

'We've got plenty of time really.' Tom sat, getting his breath back. 'They'll be about an hour in there.'

But after a short rest the boys rushed off again, and soon they were sweeping down the side of the hill towards the canal on the other side of the tunnel.

Mr Langley was in his little wooden office which was by the entrance of the tunnel — he waved to the boys and they went down to him. The first boat had already come through, and the other two followed on close behind.

'They always stick close together.' Mr Langley grinned at Bev. 'Don't want to be alone when Kit Cluckbucket starts her tricks.' He watched the third boat leave the tunnel and closed his office. 'Well, that's another day over. You boys coming back yet?'

They decided that as Tom's boat was still tied up alongside they would have a few turns at rowing up and down.

'Right, but come and get your lifejackets first,' Tom's father ordered.

Mike and Terry went off first and Tom and Bev stood on the towpath by the side of the last boat that had come through the tunnel. Two men were sitting on the deck fishing.

'Hallo, didn't we see you at the other end of the tunnel?' said one of them.

Bev and Tom told them about their race. 'We would have beaten you easily, but Bev got lost.'

'Well, I'm not as lucky as you, I don't live on top of the tunnel,' said Bev.

'Is that your place?' asked the man, pointing to Tom's house.

'Yes, my dad's the tunnel keeper.'

The other man looked up from his fishing.

'I wonder if he ought to know about —' he broke off, and his companion nodded saying to Tom, 'We heard a noise behind us in the tunnel, we thought it was another boat, but we didn't hear any engine.'

'What sort of noise?' asked Tom.

'Very hard to say exactly, our own engine sounded very loud in there, and what with the other two boats in front — but we certainly had the feeling that something or someone was behind us — well at least for part of the way, and then it suddenly stopped.'

Bev's eyes were shining with excitement. 'It was the tunnel ghost — did you smell bacon and eggs?'

'Bacon and eggs, of course not,' said the man.

'Ghost, what ghost?' his friend asked.

Tom told them.

'No,' was their definite answer. It was nothing like that, no screams or smells. I'm sure it was a boat, only it must have been one without an engine, and I reckon it turned back, and went out the way it came in.'

Mike and Terry now brought the boat back for Bev and Tom, and the boys took turns to row up and down the canal. Bev was pleased with his efforts, and found it much easier now to keep a straight course. When it was time to go home, Tom tied his boat up outside his dad's office. He stood silently by the mouth of the tunnel.

'What's the matter?' said Bev.

'Sshh!' Tom whispered.

A faint splash, splash, splash could be heard from the black interior of the tunnel, and then a noise, a kind of gurgling noise, followed by a shout.

'It's the ghost!' yelled Bev.

Tom caught hold of him and shook him.

'That's no ghost, there's someone inside!' He was untying his boat. 'We'd better go and have a look.'

'But the notice said we mustn't take in this kind of boat.'

'Someone may be trapped — I'm going, are you coming with me?'

'All right, wait for me,' Bev got into the boat beside Tom, who already had the oars in the water.

As soon as they were in the tunnel, Bev shivered. 'Gosh, it's cold in here! Ugh, it's leaking!'

Cold water dripped steadily down from the roof.

'Sshh!' said Tom, and he rowed slowly and quietly along.

Bev hugged himself tight to keep warm, and as his eyes became accustomed to the darkness, he could see the towpath running down one side of the tunnel.

'Why don't we leave the boat here and walk?'

'The towpath has collapsed in lots of places, it's not safe.'

Tom rowed deeper into the tunnel, and Bev, looking back, saw that the hole of daylight at the mouth had already become much smaller.

Tom stopped rowing and allowed the boat to drift, and after a while it started to move nearer and nearer to the wall.

'There must be a current pulling us over.' He sounded puzzled. 'That's impossible — unless —' He started paddling with one oar, and gave the other one to Bev.

'You paddle on your side.'

Bev did as he was told, and the boat, now almost hugging the wall, moved quickly through the water. Suddenly the wall stopped and the boat swung sharply into another tunnel!

'Crikey!' Tom gasped. 'This must be one of the passages to the old air shaft!'

Before Bev could ask any questions, a loud thud followed by a splash sounded in front of them, and the paddle dropped from Bev's hand in fright.

'W-what's that?'

'Quick, grab your paddle!' Tom tried to find it in the inky blackness, but it was too late, the swirling water had swept it away.

'I'm sorry.' Bev felt ashamed of himself.

'Never mind -- listen!'

They sat as still as they could, holding against the wall, and looked around them. They were in a very very narrow tunnel and in fact could touch both walls by stretching out their arms. As the boat drifted slowly through they once again heard noises. This time it was voices. Two men were speaking, and there were rustling noises, like paper being screwed up.

'Get on with it, stop standing about, we've got to move this lot out of here tonight,' said a voice. More scuffling noises, and the voice continued, 'And no more accidents! Thank goodness it was an empty box you dropped into this infernal canal.'

'But I'm sure there's someone out there -- I heard them!' Another voice, shaky and frightened.

'Rubbish, who on earth would be in the tunnel this time of night, and without an engine?'

'I told you I didn't like leaving the stuff here, it's haunted, has been for years!'

'My God, a grown man like you talking about ghosts!'

'You're not from round these parts, if you were you'd know about it, hundreds of people have heard her.'

'Ghost or no ghost, I'm taking this lot out of here tonight. Danny is expecting it in London tomorrow — now come on! We've just these two lots to pack.'

Tom and Bev could now see two shadowy figures moving in a small cave by the side of the tunnel. A canoe was tied up alongside.

'It's the one we saw outside at Kidsgrove!' whispered Tom.

'I think that's the fisherman I saw,' said Bev.

'They must be the burglars — look at that big box, it's like the one we saw under the bushes.'

'What shall we do? We can't lift that onto our boat by ourselves, and in any case they would see us, wouldn't they?' Bev thought hard.

Tom said, 'One of us will have to stay here and watch them, whilst we get a message out to my dad.'

'I know!'

Bev spoke out loud in excitement, and immediately they heard a cry from the frightened man in the cave.

'There it is again!'

'Nonsense! It must be a duck or a bird that has lost itself in the tunnel.... This is the last time I do any jobs with local amateurs. Danny will have to give me professionals next time.'

Tom and Bev paddled silently back to the main tunnel.

'Right!' said Tom. 'What's your plan?'

'Why don't we untie their canoe and tow it back to the junction, here to this very spot, and I can wait in it while you take your boat back to fetch your dad. You're much better than me at rowing and would be quicker.'

'OK! Let's hope they've used the right knot to tie up the canoe. If it's a clove hitch then it will be easy. Now keep quiet.'

They manoeuvred the boat back by pushing against the wall with their hands.

'Ugh, the wall is slippery and cold!' whispered Bev.

'Lie low,' said Tom. 'Our shadows will be shown up by their lamp.'

A man came to the edge of the cave and peered down towards them.

'I can still hear something!'

The other man joined him, and Bev could now definitely recognise the angry fisherman he'd met.

'That's him!' he whispered to Tom, who nodded back.

'Probably rats,' said the fisherman. 'Now then, where's the hammer to fix this lid, have you put all your stuff in?'

The boys edged closer and could now see that the two men were putting parcels wrapped in newspaper inside the big wooden box.

'It *is* the burglars!' said Tom. 'Move over, Bev, I think I can just reach their boat!'

He leant perilously over, and stretched out.

'It's no good. Push me a bit further along.'

Bev pushed against the wall.

'That's OK — blast!'

Their boat had gone too far, and knocked into the canoe.

'What's that!' shouted one of the men running down to the edge of the cave again.

'Quick, Tom!' called Bev.

Tom's fingers found the knot, and to his relief it was a clove hitch, and could be slipped undone easily.

'Right, Bev, push hard away!'

'Look, there they are!'

'Get out of my way, man! Where are they?'

The two men were pushing each other to see who was in the tunnel with them.

'Will you get out of my way!'

It was the voice of the angry fisherman, who was now right at the edge of the cave, looking along the dark narrow tunnel.

'Where are they? Are you sure you saw someone? ....Ah, yes, there they are!'

Tom and Bev found it slow work pushing against the wall, and Tom's fingers were very cold as they held on to the rope pulling the canoe behind them. Tom looked round just in time.

'Quick!' he said. 'He's got a gun!'

At that moment there was a flash and a loud report echoed and ricocheted along the tunnel — a singing noise hissed against the wall by the side of the boys, and something splashed into the water.

'Keep down!' warned Tom. 'Leg it — like the old boatmen!'

Bev laid back in the boat and pushed against the wall with his feet.

'Quick, we're nearly there!' urged Tom.

Another shot rang out, and the noise stunned both boys into deafness for a while — but at last they reached the junction of the main tunnel. Tom showed Bev how to tie the boat to one of the old rails on the broken towpath.

'Will you be all right?' he asked. 'I'll be as quick as I can.'

'Yes,' said Bev, but he didn't feel very brave. 'Hurry up, though, I'm very cold.'

Tom paddled off in the canoe, and Bev soon lost sight

of him in the darkness — but then he saw his silhouette against the little hole of daylight at the end of the tunnel. He strained his eyes but it seemed as if Tom would never reach the entrance — it looked as if he was standing still.

A noise in the water along the smaller tunnel suddenly caught Bev's attention — he peered into the murky darkness. What on earth was it? With a shiver of fear running down his back he saw that one of the men was swimming towards him. He couldn't stay tied up and be caught; but if he pushed off back down the tunnel he would be seen against the light the same as he had seen Tom. Bev looked at the other end of the tunnel and saw that he was in fact less than halfway through, and that the light from that end was no more than a pin-hole. He untied the boat and silently pushed against the wall. The man's head could be seen against the light from the cave. He wasn't at the junction yet, so Bev had a good chance.

After a few more pushes he started to paddle down the tunnel, until he decided he was too far for the swimmer to find him. This part of the tunnel was very wet, water seeped through the bricks down the sides and it came through the roof in a steady stream. Bev was very cold and wet, and in the inky darkness he lost all idea of time. How long had Tom been gone? Half an hour? An hour? It was now very quiet and Bev wondered if the man had found another way out. Should he perhaps go back and look? He decided to count to one hundred, and if Tom wasn't back by then he would go to the junction again.

'....ninety-eight, ninety-nine, one hundred!'

Bev started paddling back, and as he did so he noticed that the light at the entrance was very dim now — it must be very late. He had nearly reached the junction, when a terrible scream rang out and echoed back and forth along the walls. Bev felt the hairs at the back of his neck stand up with fright — his mouth went dry, and he watched with horror the light disappear at the mouth of the tunnel — the opening was gradually closing up. A roaring noise started as with a loud crash the tunnel was sealed. The scream sounded again. It wasn't far away now, and Bev looked anxiously around. If only he could find out what had happened — had a rock fallen down shutting him in along with the burglars? The roaring continued, and as Bev paddled along he felt cold air coming down towards him. Suddenly a blinding white light shone out in front of him, and he saw a boat coming towards him. Another light pierced the darkness, this time from the roof of the boat, and it turned and raked the towpath.

'Here, over here!' a voice called out, and Bev saw a man clinging to a broken wooden rail on the towpath. The boat swung over to the side and someone helped the man out of the water.

'Bev! Bev!'

It was Tom!

'I'm here!' Bev yelled, and the light turned full on him. Soon Mr Langley's arms reached down and lifted Bev on board.

'Good lad! Quick, nip down inside and get those wet things off!'

After that everything seemed to happen at once. One of the policemen left the boat and took the canoe along to the cave, but the other man had gone — leaving the stolen goods still packed in the case.

'W-w-what's that roaring noise?' Bev shivered.

'It's the ventilators — this tunnel closes both entrances when boats are inside, and ventilators keep the air going through — otherwise crews might be overcome with diesel or petrol fumes.... Anyway, that's enough explanations! Here, drink this hot tea!'

A policewoman had, whilst speaking, efficiently removed Bev's wet clothes and tucked him neatly into a warm blanket as he sat upon a bunk.

'You'll hear all about it when we get you back home.'

Bev took the hot tea and was pleased when Tom came down to see him.

'You all right?' he asked.

'Yes,' said Bev. 'What's happening up there?'

'The man in the water has told the police everything. They were the burglars, and all the things they stole had been hidden in the old air shaft.'

'What about the fisherman I saw?' asked Bev.

'Now then!' It was the policewoman again, but she was smiling at them. 'You two heroes can talk later — look, we're almost out of the tunnel.'

A grinding clanking noise was heard as the entrance opened, and the boys realised they were now out of the tunnel, and almost home again.

To Bev's disgust a policeman insisted on carrying him up to the house. He grinned at Bev's annoyed expression.

'Can't have you going home with wet, muddy feet. I reckon you'll be popped into a hot bath straight away as it is.'

And that was just what happened. Tom's mother had it already waiting, and Tom and Bev shared it.

'Straight to bed, and no playing about — both of you,' Mr Langley called up to them.

'But dad?' Tom pleaded. 'Can't you come and tell Bev what happened?'

'Please,' Bev sounded very excited. 'I don't think I'll sleep until I know all the story.'

Mr Langley came upstairs and looked at the two pyjama-clad figures.

'Well, I thought you'd be too tired,' he said.

'NO!' they both shouted.

'Well then, quickly into bed!' He laughed as they scampered underneath the covers.

'Right now. First of all, I was not pleased that you took your boat into the tunnel — you should have come to me.'

He saw their crestfallen faces.

'However, things turned out splendidly!' He leant over and tousled Bev's hair. 'I'm proud of you!'

Bev smiled with relief. 'Was the fisherman the leader?'

'Not exactly — he is a top professional in the burglary world though. No, his boss was the one the police were interested in.'

'That must be Danny,' said Bev.

'Yes, he's the brains behind all the jobs. Your fisherman just does as he's told. And lucky for us, he's told us where Danny is.'

Tom spoke. 'And the other man was a local, from Tunstall, the policeman said.'

'Yes, a small-time thief who could help them out with minor details.'

'Like hiding the stuff in the old air-shaft?'

'That's right. I must say that even I didn't know you could get in and out of that. I thought they had all been closed up when we installed the ventilators.'

'Did the fisherman get out that way?' asked Bev.

'He tried!' Mr Langley smiled. 'I'd like to have seen his face when he met two policemen at the top of the shaft.'

Bev leaned back onto his pillows, and gave a great yawn.

'That's enough talking.' Mr Langley tucked the bedclothes around the boys. 'The police will be back in the morning, and you can give them all the details then.'

He turned off the light and went downstairs where Mrs Langley was preparing some supper, and had a tray with two steaming mugs of hot chocolate ready.

'They won't need these,' Mr Langley said. 'They're fast asleep already.'

He took one of the mugs and sat down.

'Come on, let's have a rest ourselves, and we won't waste these either.'

CHAPTER TEN

It was a very happy gathering around the kitchen table the next morning. Uncle Peter and Aunt Jean has returned to find that Bev and Tom were heroes. The police sergeant had been to take the final details from the boys, and with eyes shining Bev told his uncle, 'And there's a reward! The police will be writing to Mr Langley about it.'

'Well done!' said his uncle. 'I feel proud to have you for my crew — that is, if you are ready to exchange a tunnel house for a narrow boat.'

'Oh yes, I'm ready.' Bev gave his uncle an anxious look. 'But I was wondering if perhaps Tom could come with us — for a week perhaps?' he pleaded. 'He has never been on a real canal boat, and —'

'Of course, what a splendid idea!' said Aunt Jean. 'You'll let him come, won't you?' she asked Mr and Mrs Langley.

One look at Tom's face told them they could only say 'Yes'.

'Where are you heading for?' asked Mr Langley.

'The Peak Forest canal, through the tunnel, up the Macclesfield to Marple, and then along the Peak Forest to Whaley Bridge.'

'Lovely trip — lucky you, Tom!' said his father. 'Take your binoculars, the Macclesfield has beautiful views.'

By lunchtime the boys had unpacked Tom's clothes and stowed them in the cupboard in the little cabin at the front of *Ratty* — for Tom was to share Bev's room.

'I'm afraid it's not really a double bed,' said Aunt Jean. 'But we only have room for one extra bedroom — the art gallery must come first.'

'Oh, I'll fit in OK,' said Tom.

'Ready boys?' It was Uncle Peter calling out. 'Now I've two crew members to help I'll be able to sit back and just give orders!' He smiled as they came out on deck. 'OK, Bev, you undo the front rope, and Tom the back.'

Both boys stood on the deck of *Ratty* as Uncle Peter steered beneath the measuring gauge. Tom's dad was in the office, he waved goodbye as the boat disappeared into the darkness of the tunnel.

'Let me know if you smell any bacon and eggs!' he called out.

THE END

Other Belmont Publications -

"Navigator Route Planner"
The original Inland Waterway Route Planner

"from Stem to Stern" by John M Hill

A fully illustrated, practical HANDBOOK on painting your narrow boat. Taking you literally "from Stem to Stern" showing what goes where

(Format A4 - Landscape, spiral wire bound, 60 pages)

ISBN 0 905366 27 1

"Colours for Cruisers" by John M Hill

A companion to "from Stem to Stern" This fully illustrated HANDBOOK takes you, step by step, through the application of paint with the author's unique method of colour selection

(Format A4 - Landscape, spiral wire bound, 76 pages)

ISBN 0 905366 28 X

"Fenders" by Colin Jones

A fully illustrated, step by step, HANDBOOK on making your own rope fenders

(Format A4 - Portrait, spiral wire bound)

ISBN 0 905366 31 X

"Clothes of the Cut"
by Avril Lansdell   A history of canal costume